Fabioulous Pizza

Learn the tricks of a professional and
bring them to your kitchen

by

Fabio Errante

Fabioulous Pizza

Learn the tricks of a professional
and bring them in your kitchen

Copyright © 2019 by Fabio Errante

The author reserves the right to change,
add to or delete all or part of the content
without prior notice.

First paperback edition 11/2019

ISBN 978-1-6985-2361-3 (paperback)

To my sister Mari and my brother Saro,

because they ALWAYS believed.

Acknowledgements

Hey, psst, reader!

Yes, I know, you want to get your hands dirty with flour straight away, but I'd like you to read this, because it's very important to me and it's part of the whole story.

Only a few months ago, I was a frustrated pizzaiolo who felt stuck in a job, working his bum off to make someone else's money. At some point I realised I should have done something for myself, but I didn't know what, and how to do it. Then the lightbulb moment came: as obvious as it sounds, I understood I needed help.

So I started looking for a mentor. But being a lucky guy, I hit two birds with one stone and I actually found two.

James Nicholson and Jessen James are two business partners who run the Business & Marketing School here in London.

James is the geeky one, a bottomless pit of technical knowledge who brought me from being a technophobe to being totally comfortable with marketing and advertising software.

Jessen is the King Midas of business strategy, able to understand what was going on in my mind before and better than me. For him it was as easy as ABC to trace a path for me to follow if I wanted to be independent and free.

The result is greater than the sum of its parts, though. In fact, thanks to their mentorship, I was able to start "Homemade & Fabioulous" and now I offer pizza making classes, parties and events. Moreover, they encouraged me to write the book you're reading right now.

James, Jessen, thank you for being my Mentors and my Friends, this book is for you two as well.

Introduction

Pizza.

Many people's favourite food, all over the world.

Many books were written on this subject, with different levels of detail and accuracy.

Many words were spent on these books, the most common of them being probably "Neaples" and "Dean Martin". Honestly, I can't really promise I will avoid those words myself.
What I can promise instead, is that you will know a lot more about pizza making, after you read this book.

Beware though! I'm not talking about the info you would find on the average "Come into my kitchen" blog or website, where you would find more or less the same recipe, very basic and not ideal.

On the other hand, I think that you can't run if you don't learn to walk first. It wouldn't make too much sense to tell you about pre-ferments, high hydration, advanced kneading techniques and blah blah, if you still don't know the basics.

I'm referring to little details, those usually overlooked things that make your baker's life easier and your pizza better, once you know them and once you put them in place.

My goal is to let you know about all the things you should and you shouldn't do, and why. I think that if you understand the logic behind, it is going to be easier to retain the information.

I want to invite you to come with me inside a real pizzeria, to enjoy the environment I worked in for a very long time. You will see what happens there, you will come back in your kitchen with your newly acquired knowledge and you will be able to make the best possible pizza without the need to buy any tool[1] or special ingredients.

---

[1] *A scale is the only tool I would recommend, most probably you already have one in your kitchen, but it doesn't matter if you don't have one.*

1

WHAT I HAD TO DO TO LEARN

As I said, I will bring you inside a pizzeria, but you are only required to watch carefully. Luckily enough, you won't need to do what I did.

Of course I'm referring to an italian shop, where we make italian pizza, following italian traditions and shouting italian curses (which I will refrain from teaching you). I'm not saying that italian pizza is the best you will find out there. If you prefer New York or Detroit style, Chicago thin crust or Philadelphia Tomato Pie, Deep-dish or Grilled...well, I'm not even remotely thinking to change your mind.

I will talk about Italian Pizza because it's the only one I can make and because I make it good. For the sake of authenticity, the best thing you can do to learn something about italian pizza, is to deal with an italian pizzaiolo. In this case, me.

Now, consider that my career as a professional pizza maker spans seven and a half years at the time of writing.

For the first two years I worked in Italy, where we are used to work six days per week, and I had the chance to enjoy 28 days of holidays per year. This means that I worked: 6 days x 52 weeks = 312 days per year. Minus 28 days holidays, equals 284 days per year (hence 568 days in total).

I worked in two restaurants in Italy: the first one was a take-way only and we used to bake 110 to 160 pizzas during weekdays and at least 250 during weekends, with peaks of 300. Crunching these numbers, I can say that I have baked on average 201 pizzas per day in my first year of work.

The total is 201 pizzas x 284 days = 57,084 pizzas.

I worked in another restaurant, which was mainly an eat-in. The weekend was pretty busy, but the weekdays were often slow and we had one very bad Tuesday when we only sold 20 pizzas! On the other end, I still remember with dread that Saturday, in September 2013, when we baked around 400 pizzas...and I managed to survive.

By the way, these numbers were the extremes. In general we used to bake between 60 and 80 pizzas during weekdays, and 250 to 300 during weekends. This brings to an average of 163 baked pizzas per day, during a typical week.

So during my second year work I baked 168 pizzas x 284 days = 47,712 pizzas.

All together, my two years work in Italy has seen me bake a grand total of 104,796 pizzas.

Then I decided to move to London. At first I worked in a branch of a very famous fake-italian franchise. It was a short lasting experience, during which I baked another 10,460 pizzas.

Finally, I've started working at Organica Pizza, in North London, nicest place ever and best boss ever. I left almost five years later only because a new owner took over. Overall, I have worked there for 2,006 days.

It's harder to do the calculations here since the time lapse is longer, and we had several ups and downs. But I think I'm not too far away from reality if I say that I made 86 pizzas x 2,006 days = 172,516.

Ladies and gentlemen, it looks like during my whole career as a professional pizzaiolo I made...drum roll...**287,772** pizzas. Please note, I'm neither including what I have baked at home starting from the age of around twelve, nor the things I baked in the very first pizzeria I worked in, because they were still "unofficial".

All these calculations lead to more numbers, check these out.

Bags of flour unzipped: 1,610

Buckets of water poured: 4,911

Sachets of yeast ripped: 41,110

Bags of salt used: 144

Cans of tomatoes opened: 10,359

Mozzarella balls cut: 230,217

Basil leaves plucked: 863,316

Olive oil bottles unscrewed: 25,899

Mushrooms sliced: 43,166

Pineapples *sigh* peeled: 479

Fingers and hand cuts: 21

Light burns self-caused: 12

Scars still visible: 3

Deaths: half

Beers stolen when the owner wasn't in: erm...none

Wow, that's a lot of stuff, it seems like I have worked hard. But I'm not complaining, in the end I had to learn, right?

2

MY BIGGEST MISTAKE

The first place where I learnt about pizza making was my Mom's kitchen. In the house I grew up in we had a tradition: every Saturday night all the five members would gather around the kitchen table, facing a huge chunk of homemade pizza.

My mom was usually the pizza maker in charge but, from time to time, I was allowed to do my part. Maybe just open a can of tomatoes, or chop some mozzarella, or dissolve the yeast in water. Until one day, finally, I had the chance to do everything by myself. Under Mamma's watchful eye, of course.

Following the directions of my mom and the recipe of my grandma, I was able to prepare a decent dough from scratch. Then I stretched it, then I put the toppings and then I baked it.

Ladies and gentlemen, Saturday's dinner is ready, and I made it myself.

I made that first pizza at the age of twelve, and it felt great! I even told my dad that I was going to be a pizzaiolo, as a grown up, but of course he laughed at me and told me I would become an architect or an engineer.

By the way, having made that first pizza didn't mean that I became the official pizzaiolo of the house. But, you know, to my kid's eyes my career officially kick-started that very day.

To be honest, it took a long time before I had the chance to make pizza from scratch again, but every Saturday I was still there, beside my mother, helping her as usual and gaining more and more confidence in my skills.

Eventually, over time the roles between me and my mom basically reversed. This happened so slowly I didn't even notice. I wish I had an official investiture ceremony and a special prize for my patience, but all I received was the wooden board instead. Only a few years later I realised how precious it was.

Fast forward twenty years later...

Eventually I reached a point where I had baked plenty of pizzas at home, collected relatives', friends' and neighbours' recipes, read several cookbooks with tips about pizza-making, saved on my bookmarks a fair amount of links to pizza related websites - at that time, the internet was still young but you could still find quite a few sources.

In short, I thought I knew everything there was to know about pizza making but today I know I was a bit too confident. So when I entered Mario's pizzeria for the first time, I thought that I would have been able to serve the first pizza to a customer in a matter of a few days - if not a few hours. How bloody wrong I was...

But wait, who's this Mario guy?

My second, but most important learning place, was the pizza shop I used to buy take away from and its owner's name was precisely Mario[2]. He was the main pizza maker and I became his friend pretty quickly, since he cooked my dinner at least once a week.

From time to time, while I was waiting for my pizza, I used to ask my new friend to teach me some trick or to explain to me some "behind the scene". I asked once, I asked twice. Mario always replied to me with the same words "Whenever

---

[2] *No, he's not a plumber, he doesn't have a moustache and he doesn't have a brother called "Luigi".*

you want, I would be happy to teach you". But I never took him seriously. Actually I didn't even take myself seriously, I was only shooting sentences.

Until one day...

"Mario, your pizza is way better than the one I make myself, you should explain to me how the heck you do it!"

"Ok, Fabio, you always ask but you never listen to me. The fact is, I could really use two extra hands. Would you come and help me here? I won't pay you a cent, but I'll teach you all you need to become a real pizzaiolo. Moreover, you will eat pizza every night. You will cook it yourself."

"Yes, when can I start?"

The very next day, at the end of my usual shift, I officially entered the pizza-making wonderland.

My first experience in a restaurant was like going back in time to the age of twelve, with Mario playing the role of my mom. Probably this went a little bit too far, because while he was explaining what to do next, I often would look at him and picture him with my mom's haircut, spectacles and even with her skirt!

It took me a while to admit it to myself, and It was hard to do it, but the truth was that everything I knew about pizza was only a teeny, tiny fraction of what I would need to know if I wanted to become a professional. I had to deal with the fact that, no matter how much you know, there will always be somebody that knows more than you do.

I guess this lesson was useful outside of the restaurant too.

Here's the biggest mistake I made during that experience: I thought I knew a lot, but I didn't. However, this did not throw me down, indeed it stimulated me a lot! Being a very curious guy, I was excited to put on my student hat again and I was ready to learn all the new concepts that I would be taught from that day on.

***

The very first thing that was clear to me, was that I should have learnt to do my shopping correctly. Whenever I felt like making pizza in my house, which used to happen pretty often, I was interested in the toppings I would have used more than anything else. So I would have headed to the supermarket to grab a random bag of flour, a random tomato-y thing, etc. Now I know that to make a very good pizza an extra effort is needed. Not a big one though, just learn the difference between the different types of flour, this is the starting point. Of course we will not talk here about the flours used by professionals in their restaurants, we will only point out what we need to know to make a good pizza in our home.

Think about how many kinds of flour you know: plain, self raising, wholemeal, gluten free. And then soya, rice, spelt, corn, semolina, you name it. They are different from each other and you could use them in different ways and recipes, including pizza.

However, when we first approach the shelf at the supermarket and reach out to grab a bag of flour, there is only ONE big difference we need to consider. Did you ever even notice? You see "strong" and "very strong" written on some bags, most of the times it's "bread flour". If none of these two characteristics is written, then that particular flour is "weak". This is the case of "Plain" or "All Purpose" flour.

Please note that different countries use different classification names for the flour. Many aspiring pizza makers worldwide are aware of the "00" flour, usually referred to as the best flour you can use to make pizza at home.

However, "00" is just a name we Italians use for a certain type of flour. We classify the flour according to its degree of refinement, from higher to lower: type 00, 0, 1, 2 and wholemeal. But this is not enough to understand if the product is or isn't good to bake a good pizza, as we still need to know how "strong" the flour is.

That's why, in this book, I will only refer to the categories mentioned above. The weak versus strong flour question is very important for us. We must consider it first and foremost because different strength means different time: the stronger the flour, the longer we will be allowed to wait for the dough to be ready to be cooked. In fact, a stronger flour will produce a greater amount of gluten, which will trap the gas produced by the yeast for longer, so our dough will rise nice and high.

Would this be of any help?

Why would we want to be allowed more rising time for our dough?

There are two main reasons.

First of all, your pizza will be easier to stretch when the time to bake comes. Dough's components such as sugars, starches and proteins themselves need time to break down into simpler elements. We refer to this decaying action as "maturation".

If we give our dough enough time to mature, our base won't put up much resistance. Moreover, this process will affect in a positive way the digestibility of our final product. Hence, also our stomach's job will be smoother, not only ours.

The second reason why we want our dough to rise longer is because we need some "fermentation".
Now, knowing all the chemistry behind the fermentation process is beyond the scope of this book. For the purpose of home bakers like us, it's enough to know that, thanks to fermentation, the dough will develop a slightly acidic touch. This will turn into taste and flavour when we will bake.

The different strength will also affect the amount of water absorbed by the flour: starting with the same amount of water, a strong flour will absorb more than a weak flour, consequently you would use, on average, around 6%-7% less.

This feature is extremely overlooked.

Many recipes do not specify the kind of flour you should use. Or worse, they say you can use any flour. That's why your pizza is different every time you make it, even though you always follow the same recipe to the letter. Most probably you just bought a different flour.

By bringing these info into our household's kitchen, you will be able to prepare a better pizza, assessing what to do, when and why.

The starting point is that you should give our dough much more time to rise than the most common recipes suggest we do. Also, you must manage your time differently depending on the kind of flour we want to use.

As an indication, we can consider that plain/all purpose flour matures in three to four hours after you finish kneading, being weak. A strong flour will take eight to ten hours instead. Finally, a very strong flour would easily take twenty-four hours to mature and you would not be wrong at all to wait longer, even two days, three or more.

Please consider that these timings are just approximations, but they will help you to fit the pizza preparation in your schedule.

Personally, I wouldn't suggest using plain flour for your homemade pizza. By the time it will be mature it will not be fermented enough, hence it will be less tasty.

You might think "Ok then, I'm going to wait longer so my dough will be fermented enough". The problem is that, at that point, the dough will be really mature. As a consequence its consistency will be really soft and it will not be easy to stretch a nice pizza evenly.

"Evenly" it's the keyword here: the dough would indeed increase its size very easily because of its weakness, but you would likely mark dips and pits and holes on your base.

You need to become more experienced to handle a soft dough and stretch an even base.

In the meanwhile just use strong flour.

Thanks to the longer time it will allow us, we will be able to reach the right balance between maturation and fermentation without ending up with a brittle dough ball. If you wanted to, you could even knead today and bake tomorrow, just like we do it in most pizzerias - as a matter of fact, I recommend to proceed this way, that's actually how I often do it myself.

Discovering all of these subtleties was a real light bulb moment.

But it was only the first one, followed by many others that I will share with you.

***

Now, my favourite pizza was always Margherita[3]. The simplest and the best, with just two ingredients: a bit of tomato and a bit of mozzarella.

I'm not particularly fond of pizzas with plenty of toppings. The greatest achievement for a pizzaiolo is to make a good dough and if you cover it with stuff it's unlikely you will tell the nice from the crappy one.
Besides, I like being able to distinguish and identify different flavours, and if I have too many in my mouth, my taste buds get confused.

Maybe that's just because I'm italian: you probably know that most of our traditional recipes are very simple and we often use just two or three ingredients. But if the result is a (giant) plate of *Pasta alla carbonara* or, indeed, a *Pizza Margherita*...well...I don't miss anything extra.

---

[3] *Please note, the correct spelling is "Margherita", while the wrongly used "Margarita" refers to a nice cocktail. This pizza was named after the Queen of Italy by the then famous pizzaiolo Raffaele Esposito, who had the honour to serve it at the Sovereigns' court.*

By the way, since Margherita is such a simple one, to transform "her" into something special you need to take special care of her components, tomato and mozzarella, as said earlier.

Let's start with tomato.

During my journey through homebaking, my obvious choice was a simple jar of tomato passata. And that was for two reasons: first of all because I've always seen something that looked like passata on my pizza, when I ate out or when I had take-away.

But of course I was interested in the practical matter too: basically you open a jar and you're good to go, just add a pinch of salt.

I had my favourite brands and they tasted slightly different, but beside the consistency or maybe the colour, I always had to admit that the restaurant-made pizza I was eating was topped with a better tasting tomato.

Before I took my first step into the magical world of professional pizza making, I assumed it was because restaurants had access to better quality products, some kind of special things I wouldn't have been able to find on the high street.

But I was wrong once again.

In fact, the very first time I saw tomatoes in the pizzeria I was working in, I noticed they were branded with a famous name, very common to find on the shelves of the supermarkets, still nowadays.

Much to my surprise! Because actually I had bought that very same brand more than once, but on top of my homemade pizza it tasted just different. After a closer look, I had the chance to spot the apparently subtle difference: they weren't chopped tomatoes, they were whole peeled tomatoes.
Bam!

How's that possible? They taste so different, but they are the same brand and, in the end, they are just bloody tomatoes!
Well, you just have to think that, in order to produce passata, a long and complex procedure is necessary. You need to:

1) harvest the tomatoes;
2) peel them;
3) cut them:
4) remove the seeds;

5) chop them;

6) add their own water;

7) heat them to a high temperature (often 100° degrees);

8) bottle the final product.

To produce peeled tomatoes, you clearly stop at number two.

I'm not aware of the finest details of the processes that lie behind the industrial production, but I think it's safe to say that peeled tomatoes are way less processed than passata.

And that's the reason why they taste better - wow, it seems so obvious to me today.
Now that you know what's the difference, do yourself a favour and buy only peeled tomatoes. You don't need to search every supermarket and every website to find the famous San Marzano tomatoes, unless you want to try them because they are the only ones allowed by the true Neapolitan tradition.

You don't even need to look for the higher price tag. Just buy peeled tomatoes and taste the difference yourself, for a start. Then, when and if you feel like exploring new territories, see if you want to make the extra effort to try something better.

I bet that you're now curious to know how professionals transform those peeled tomatoes into the delicious base they spread on top of their pizza.

Of course I'm here to please you, that's why I will reveal to you another insider secret and I will tell you the exact recipe to prepare the tomato sauce, the very same I follow in the pizzeria.

Here we go: open a can of peeled tomatoes, chop them roughly with a fork or even with your hands, add salt to taste.

Done.

This is really the most basic and authentic recipe, there is no secret sauce in the tomato sauce (pun intended, sorry). It's a simple preparation, just like many others of the italian cooking style.
Yes, sure, many add basil, some add extra virgin olive oil, but there's no need to add herbs, garlic, "italian" seasoning, freshly ground black pepper, pink himalayan salt, ginger root harvested on the Everest plateau.

Ok I just made this last one up, but you get the point, you don't really need to add anything but a pinch of salt, if you are after an "authentic" italian pizza sauce.

And here's the icing on the cake: you don't even need to cook. There is a common conception about using "Marinara" which, to my knowledge, is a sauce cooked with onions and/or garlic, herbs and other stuff.

I can say without fear of contradiction that this is not traditional at all.

Even though I had the chance to meet one colleague who prefers to cook its tomato sauce, he represents the proverbial exception that confirms the rule and he is perfectly aware that he's doing something "different".

Most professional pizza-makers like to top their pizzas with raw tomato sauce, I am definitely one of them and I will always endorse this practice.
However, I'm not here to stop you if your palate calls for cooked tomato sauce, rather than raw. On the contrary, I'm here to grant you my very special permission to do whatever you want with your food!

I just hope that what happened to me several years ago never happens to you: a clumsy move made me drop from my hands the container where I had just prepared fifteen kilos of sauce.

FIFTEEN KILOS.

Now they were on the floor. And it was almost opening time. Good thing I never cooked tomato sauce, it only took me an extra five minutes to make again the whole batch - please, allow me to overlook the time I needed to clean up after my own mess, bad things may happen after all!

Once I have learnt this unexpected breakthrough about tomatoes, I would have only needed to know something about the last ingredient of my Margherita, if I want "her" spread the wings and fly happily to the next level.

Luckily enough, the lesson was right behind the corner and of course it was about mozzarella, pizza cheese "par excellence".
The recipe of the old Neapolitan tradition[4] calls for either buffalo or cow mozzarella.

However, nowadays the preferred cheese used by restaurants is the variety called "Fiordilatte", literally it means "Flower of milk". It has less moisture than ordinary

---

[4] *As stated by the "Disciplinare", the document which contains the written rules to make the original Neapolitan Pizza.*

mozzarella and this helps to avoid the "pool effect" on your pizza.

But this characteristic of fiordilatte is not enough to avoid a watery pizza. When I was baking at home I always bought Fiordilatte for my masterpieces, because I wanted to feel like a pro. Regardless, my pizzas always ended up having a little pond in the middle...I should have thought to use some fishy topping, they would have appreciated all that water.

At some point I tried to do something about it, precisely I dried the mozzarella slices using several sheets of kitchen towels. However, this wasn't enough, I still got watery pizzas.

What's more, I always had to double check that some piece of paper had not remained attached to the slices of mozzarella and, if that was the case, surgically remove those white-on-white things. I think I ate plenty of kitchen tissue though, good thing paper is biodegradable.
What do we do in the pizzeria instead?

It is standard practice to prepare everything in advance, because of course you better stay glued to the work table during the service. The mozzarella is treated in different ways depending on its format and according to the preferences of the pizza maker.

There are those who cut it roughly into pieces with a knife and those who use special machines. Several chefs prefer to buy it already diced, to save time. In any case, the common element is the water that collects on the bottom of the container over time. This time can be quite long, it takes a while for the mozzarella to dry enough.

The way we work in the pizzeria suggests once again how to behave at home, here's what you need to do: cut or dice the mozzarella well in advance and do it several hours before you need it.

For example, you could do it early in the afternoon if you plan to have pizza for dinner, but doing it in the morning will work even better. And you can even do it the previous day if you want to minimise the chance to see even the smallest droplet on your pizza.

In any case, I would suggest leaving the mozzarella in a colander so the water will slowly drip away. And don't forget to leave the colander itself inside a bowl, otherwise you will end up with a nice milky pond on your table, or on your kitchen's floor.

This method is useful if you use either proper, real mozzarella or fiordilatte, since they are both moist and they need some special care.

However, on the shelves at the supermarket, I see plenty of different products called "mozzarella". They are often grated, shredded or sliced, often with a yellow-ish colour and they are fairly dry so you can use them straight away.

Keep in mind that, even though we like them, more often than not they are not legit products, they are just a cheese whose taste is more or less similar to that of mozzarella.

Again, if you are not particularly interested in authenticity, just use them. I did it myself once, I think it was 1997, so I would forgive you.

***

So far we have already learnt a lot about some of the main components of a pizza, namely flour, tomato and mozzarella. At this point we are already able to consciously buy the ingredients of my favourite, my beloved Margherita. Furthermore, we know how to manage them and treat them in the best way.

Clearly this is not enough! Before we can put our new knowledge to good use, we need to shape a nice dough ball. But this is a different story and we will read about it in the next chapter.

3

I KNEAD PIZZA

My mother had this beautiful wooden board, inherited from her mom, who had it made to measure by a carpenter.

She worked all her dough by hand on top of this board, starting with some flour right in the middle, measuring by eye. Then she poked a hole into the flour and poured the liquid ingredients: eggs in the case of fresh pasta, water when making pizza.

The latter case is the one we are more interested in right now, obviously!

She first heated a little bit of water using a small pot and then added some fresh yeast. In Italy it's very common[5] and it's usually sold in cubes weighing 25 grams.

---

[5] *Fresh yeast is harder to find elsewhere, but that's no big deal, you can use dried yeast and still have excellent results.*

My mom always used a whole one, she dissolved it using a teaspoon and then poured the mixture on the flour, as said before. In this phase, she used to add salt too.

The not-so-funny part was when the water started to overflow from its flour "basin" and it was necessary to catch it before it fell from the board...On a second thought, it was actually quite funny to watch my mother's expressions when she was trying to solve the situation!

By the way, when there were no more torrents in sight, she started kneading and kneading until the dough wasn't sticky anymore.

To help herself with this, she used to add some extra flour little by little. Eventually, when she finished kneading and the dough was ready, its consistency was pretty firm and sometimes it was not too smooth. At that point, it was time to let the dough leaven.

Usually it took about an hour to rise and reach the right size, which is supposed to be at least twice the original. However, the wait was often a couple of hours, sometimes it was longer and some other times, the really bad ones, the disaster happened: the dough did not rise at all, much to my mom's great dismay.

This was pretty much the very same procedure I followed for a long time and I experienced myself different dough textures, different rising times and different, untold curses when something went wrong.

Good for me, the issues I encountered became less and less, as in the following years I have studied a lot and I learnt many lessons on my own. But the best part came when I got into the pizzeria and the experienced professionals I had the luck to work with, taught me many more lessons.

I learnt one of the earliest lessons, and probably the first one related to the preparation of the dough, during my very first day as an apprentice. It was a lucky occurrence, because often the master pizza makers are quite jealous of their recipe and they are reluctant to share it with anybody, let alone the new kid on the block who just came into their shop. Instead, I've seen my teacher making his dough straight away, he actually showed me the procedure and described to me everything he was doing, and why.

So how does a professional make his dough?

First of all he does his calculations. We pizzaioli know that, for each litre of water we use, we will get a certain number of dough balls, often twelve if you consider the average weight of each of them. And twelve is also the number of dough balls that will fit inside the typical trays[6] employed in the pizzeria.

Basically, professionals just try to make their life easier, so let's follow their example when making pizza at home.

You will see later on, that the recipe we will use involves using 100 grams of water per person, as an easy number to remember and an easy way for us to do our calculations and figure out how much flour we will need. Please note that this will be the exact, total amount of flour we will use: never an extra gram, rather one less.

Recipes give exact doses for a reason, we don't want to change them or alter their balance.

Besides, another good reason why I like to start with water when I make pizza in my kitchen, is that the process certainly seems simpler, quicker and cleaner to me. I use a bowl, so all the dough remains inside it. No particular attention is necessary, since those sudden water overflows would be impossible. Little rivers of water, flowing outside of the flour all over my board and possibly on my floor, I don't fear you anymore, HA!

---

[6] *Usually their size is 60 x 40 cm.*

Let's start with water then, and let's use it as it comes out of the tap: room temperature, without needing to heat it, as this could lead to some problems if we are not careful.

We only need one requirement, it has to be drinkable.

Although I have met people saying that the secret to making a good pizza is water, I think that this affirmation has no rational foundation whatsoever. The water is tasteless and, even if its content in mineral salts can vary, as well as its pH, this does not affect in a significant way the quality or taste of the slice you're biting, so there is no reason why we should be particularly interested in these details.

Let me widen the topic for one moment: there are a few liquids that you can use, either as a replacement for water or as an addition.

One of them is sparkling water and this makes sense: the bubbles are made by adding carbon dioxide, that is the very same gas produced by yeast's breathing. This could help the leavening and some say that it gives a crunchier texture to the crust.

The same concept is behind the use of beer. Plus, remember that beer itself contains actual yeast, although in small amounts. Finally, it has a flavour of its own and this will certainly give your pizza a different taste.

We could even use milk, but we would enter a different territory here!

Although I can't exclude that there are professional pizza makers using milk in their dough, I've never had the chance to meet any of them. However, milk is commonly used in bread making and it is known to make your final product nice and soft. If you aim to give fluffiness to your homemade pizza, you can consider substituting half of the water with milk.

If you feel like daring...use milk only.

You can expect a different, richer flavour too, due to the extra fat you are introducing. I did a couple of experiments but the result wasn't *my* cup of tea, maybe I'm too ordinary.

Last but not least, a word about olive oil, since many pizza makers use it in their dough and I did it myself on many occasions. I want to mention it here because we're talking about liquids, but obviously you're not going to prepare a dough with olive oil instead of water.

It is considered rather as an additive and you can use it to get certain features, if you are looking for them: your dough would be more extensible and flexible, your pizza would develop a slightly bigger volume and would be softer. If you plan to use olive oil in your dough, there is a right time to add it, you will read about it further in the book. For now, make a note to self, we would only use Extra Virgin Olive Oil (EVO).

But it's time to come back to our dough, now!

Once the water has been poured into your bowl or mixer, it's time to add the ingredient that will make a difference, the yeast. Without it our dough would not rise at all and, if you tried to cook it, you would only get a flat, not-so-soft , sad disk and you would not enjoy eating too much.

So we need yeast for its ability to let our dough rise, right? But how is that possible?

Remember that yeast is a biological entity, it belongs to the "Fungus" family and you would easily find it in the environment, in its free state[7]. While it carries out its

---

[7] Legend has it that an Egyptian slave, carried away by her duties, forgot her dough on the table. When she finally returned, she found a big, fluffy mass, much to her surprise. Since her master was already impatient, she baked what she had and the result was awesome: a lighter, softer bread her master found delicious. From that day on, she always "forgot" her dough on her table!

metabolism it produces some gas, in particular carbon dioxide, just like us.

As we have created a nice gluten network, thanks to the proteins in our flour and the strength in our mighty arms, the dough will rise because the gas has no chance to go anywhere. We refer to this process as "leavening" or "proofing".

One of the main differences between what we do in the pizzeria and what the average home cook does, lies in the way yeast is used, or rather in the used quantity.

I bet that, googling pizza dough recipes, you stumbled upon these doses: 500 grams of flour and "one level tablespoon" dried yeast, usually around fifteen grams. Or maybe "one sachet", around seven grams...slightly better, but still not good enough.

Also, the typical recipe recommends dissolving the yeast in warm or lukewarm water. Furthermore, it is often suggested to add sugar to "help" the yeast.

With these amounts and these conditions, once the yeast will start doing its thing, it will do it pretty fast. The leavening process would accelerate too much and the dough would double up its size quickly, typically between forty-five minutes and one hour.

Do you remember what I said about the maturation and fermentation of the dough? I said it takes time, we are talking about hours here. But despite this, someone is now telling you to speed up the process by three or four times, best case scenario.

In substance, it is suggested to make a plain, bland dough, reluctant when you stretch it and probably a bit harder to digest.

If the right amount of yeast is not the one indicated by the manufacturer's direction for use, how much should we use then?

Well, there is no hard and fast rule, as we will always need to consider that important extra factor that is the temperature of our room.

But, as we will see later on, we can manage the temperature somehow, so let's stick to a rule of thumb for our purpose: using up to 450/500 grams of flour, you will add only ONE gram of yeast. Up to 900/1000 grams of flour you will add TWO grams of yeast and so on.

If you are not already familiar with my "Fabioulous Dough Calculator", then head to bit.ly/doughcalculator using your favourite internet browser, and take advantage of this simple free tool, it will tell you the exact doses you need.

Finally, let's become familiar with the two most common kinds of yeast we find on the shelves of the supermarket.

You will find the "active" and the "instant" yeast, often referred to as "quick action", "fast action", or something related to the speed of its activity. They are both dried through an industrial process, very aggressive in the case of "active" yeast, a little less in the case of "instant". This implies a slightly different way of using them, as you will see in a moment.

The active yeast comes in small granules, which are simply cells of yeast covered by starch. The manufacturer always suggests activating it in water, where the starch will dissolve and the actual yeast will be released. Often the addition of a pinch of sugar is recommended.

The instant yeast comes in tiny sticks and it doesn't need any special treatment, you can use it straight away. It's usually recommended to sprinkle it onto the flour, since it will start its activity once it will meet the water - or the liquid.

These are pretty much the same kind of yeast we use in many pizza shops here in London, where I live at the moment. I am pretty happy with the results I get with dried yeast to the point that, even if fresh yeast was easier to find, I'm not 100% sure I would use it. Probably I would only do it to be respectful of the tradition I used to follow in Italy.

However, try and find it if you want, maybe they use it in your favourite bakery and you can ask them if they can sell you a little piece. If you manage to find it, keep in mind that you should use 3x the amount of dried yeast you would use in your recipe.

***

We are halfway through. Two out of four ingredients are already there, now we only need to add some flour and a pinch of salt.

There is a method most pizza makers follow when they prepare the dough and we will try to replicate it at home.

We're going to add the flour in several rounds, the first will be the bigger one. If you're using a stand mixer, it's ok to add half to one third of the total amount of flour.

If you're kneading by hand, then it's ok to add just half of the flour.

In this phase we are trying to build up a layer to keep the yeast separated from the salt. Those two are not exactly best friends, that's why we will add salt only after the aforementioned protective layer is built.

You are probably wondering why we have to keep them separate.

The answer lies in salt's ability to absorb moisture from the surrounding environment, including nearby cells of yeast, in our case. Salt is "hygroscopic", and if we put it in direct contact with yeast, it could easily kill its cells absorbing their water. But obviously we can't do without salt.

Besides its obvious function of giving more taste, salt offers many benefits:

1) it grants elasticity and reduction of the stickiness;
2) it provides resistance to our dough;
3) it slows down both the microbial activity and the enzymes responsible for the softening;
4) it makes the gluten network stronger;
5) it will improve volume, softness, fragrance and colour.

As you can see, even something we take for granted in our everyday cooking, can have such a meaningful impact.

If you feel a little bit like playing the chemist, do this experiment: grab two glasses and pour some water in them, filling them up to half.

I would suggest speeding up the things using lukewarm water, so you will see the outcome in around ten minutes.

Then add half a teaspoon of yeast and the same amount of sugar in both glasses. Finally, add half a teaspoon of salt in one glass only and wait to see what happens.

I don't want to spoil the surprise, so I will not describe the result, but you will see what I mean when I say that salt has a bad influence on the activity of the yeast.

I always do this little experiment during my pizza making classes and, without fail, I see many surprised expressions on the faces of the attendees. I also shot a video, it's a time lapse that lasts only a couple of minutes, so you won't have to wait for the magic thing to happen in real time.

To watch it just copy this link on your favourite browser: bit.ly/yeastexperiment.

Let's go back to kneading.

Now that we've added a first round of flour and a nice layer is built, we can add salt to our dough. The most common dose is 2% of the amount of flour. It's not strictly necessary to let the dough absorb the salt completely before we continue, we can add more flour straight away and finish it in two or three rounds.

As obvious as it sounds, please always remember to add salt.

If you don't, you will end up with a gooey, gluey mass and you would have to fix it. But adding salt at that point will give you hard times, as you would need a good effort and strong arms to incorporate it nicely into the dough.

This is the point at which things get harder, or funnier, depending on your point of view. You have to transform a mass still lacking a well-defined shape into a beautiful ball of dough, nice and smooth, soft and non-sticky.

You will need time, patience and a bit of elbow grease...unless you've got a stand mixer, then you will only need time.

If you have a mixer, use its "Hook" tool as it's very similar to what we use in most pizzerias, where the most common kind of professional mixer boasts a nice spiral-shaped tool that kneads pretty nicely.

There is a reason why, to produce a nice dough, these machines spin in the same direction[8]: it's easier to create the gluten network we want.

If you knead by hand, you should avoid squeezing, squashing, stretching, pushing, twisting and so on...they are not good for our purpose. The dough enjoys repeating movements, so find one that comes natural and flowing for you, then repeat it over and over, keeping momentum.

You could try and get familiar with a certain movement I find pretty effective and I use myself when I knead by hand: put your fingers underneath the dough and fold it on itself from the bottom up, maybe with a little help by your thumb. You want to push the edge you're handling into the centre of the dough ball. Then rotate your dough 90 degrees and repeat the movement with another side of the dough ball. Then rotate your dough 90 degrees and repeat the movement.

---

[8] *Actually some professional mixers can reverse the kneading direction, but that's a feature only needed for particular purposes.*

Then rotate your dough 90 degrees and repeat the movement again...

This could be demanding and tiring if you are dealing with big amounts and preparing a big dinner for a family gathering or a pizza party with friends, but it will be rewarding too.

Remember, there is always somebody who is in a worse position, for example yours truly when he had to face a broken mixer...and you can imagine how many dough balls we need to make ready in the pizzeria, right? After I kneaded around 18 kilos of water and flour, I could barely feel my arms, and I still had to do my daily preparation...Busy day, that one!

Enough with my adventures, we have things to do here.

If you are kneading by hand, be aware of a very common, lethal mistake people make during this phase: work on a floured surface.

Actually that's even suggested by many recipes, blogs, websites. I can't get my head around this and I absolutely don't understand why, it could totally ruin your dough!
In fact, if you get in the habit of dusting your working surface with flour to reduce the stickiness, I am sure you

will do it repeatedly as the dough absorbs the flour and starts to become sticky again.

The problem is, you will end up altering completely the balance of the recipe you're following and it's extremely likely that your dough will be hard, dry, it will not have a smooth surface and it will not even stick together. Furthermore, when it's time to stretch it, you will see how reluctant it will be. It will tend to shrink back and you'll have to be very patient to stretch it to the size you want.

So please mark these words: it's extremely important that you resist the temptation to add more flour.

Do not worry if the dough is a bit sticky, that's normal. Keep kneading! The further you go, the less sticky it will become, and when it won't be sticky anymore, that's actually the first signal that your dough could be ready.

If you are using a mixer, you will notice that the dough comes off the walls of the bowl easily. Then you can do a quick and easy test, pressing gently the tip of your finger on the dough. If it springs back to its original shape, then it's ready, otherwise you will need to work a bit more.

A different, a bit more complicated method, it's the "windowpane" test: let your dough rest for a minute or two, then take a piece and flatten it. Spread it apart with your fingers, slowly and gently, until you get a thin "window" that you can see through. If it rips, then the dough is not properly kneaded yet and you want to spend a couple more minutes on it.

In the pizzeria we don't actually use any of these tests. Professionals look for something called "punto di pasta" roughly translated as "dough point". It's the right combination of elements you catch with your touch and eyesight, and every pizza maker looks for his very own punto di pasta.

Once we finished kneading, a whole new chapter starts, both for our dough and for this book. But before you turn the page, let me give you a last word of advice.

If you plan to prepare several pizzas, you should knead one big batch of dough and THEN break it down into equal parts. Probably this will seem pretty obvious for some of you, but I don't want to take anything for granted.

In fact, once I saw with my own eyes a photo of a person kneading several pizzas in different bowls, each with their own water, yeast, flour and salt. This is terribly time consuming and I would strongly recommend avoiding it.

4

WHILE YOU WAIT

I would say that the physically hardest part is done and for the next phase we will need to use our brains rather than our arms. Our dough ball is finally ready and it only needs to stand by for a while, until it's ready to be stretched and baked. As you already know by now, this waiting time will be different, depending on the kind of flour you used.

Here's a quick recap table for you:

Flour	Waiting time
Plain/All purpose	3-4 hours
Strong/bread	8-10 hours
Very strong/bread	24+ hours

The overall waiting time will be split in two.

Let me be more specific about this.

Even though I've made pizza just for myself once (this is the official version, please do not tell my girlfriend, she would dump me), the most likely occurrence was that I made at least a couple. And since we now know that it's not very time-effective to knead several times, let's take for granted that we have prepared just one big dough ball.

Once we finished kneading, the dough will start its first fermentation[9], so we should let it rest for a while before we do something else. Each and every pizza maker let the dough do its first fermentation for a different time, but I have never met anyone who would wait less than half an hour.

We will do the same at home, following the footsteps of the professionals in the same fashion we did so far: my suggestion is to let your dough rest for one whole hour.

I would leave it inside a bowl, or a container of any kind. It's important to keep it covered, although you don't necessarily need an airtight lid/cover. Even a simple damp cloth would do the job.

---

[9] *A curious fact: in Italian we refer to this phase using the word "Puntata", which is the same word we use for "Episode".*

All we have to do at this point is to keep the dough safe from draughts and puffs, otherwise its surface will dry. A dry surface could easily hinder the leavening and would make it harder to stretch your pizza later on, so take care.

When one hour has passed, it's time to cut the dough into equal parts. We absolutely don't want to knead the new, smaller dough balls once again. We will only shape them gently and quickly, in just a few seconds. We want to make them nice and round, so it should be easier for our final product to be also round, or at least round-ish.

Now that we have a few dough balls which only need to rise, there's nothing else to do for us but wait. Since the first hour is already gone, we will subtract it from the overall waiting time indicated on the table above. So if for example you're using plain flour, you will have to wait two to three hours.

However, there's a plot twist here.

I will let you have one more peek inside the pizzeria and share the way we pizza makers work. Once we have already split our dough into as many balls as we need according to our calculations, we will not use them on the very same day. We will put them in the fridge and we will start to use them the day after[10].

There is a logic behind this practice.

I'm sure you are by now familiar with the concept of "maturation" of the dough, the process during which sugars, starches and proteins will break down into simpler elements. And of course you knew about the leavening/proofing process before you started reading this book.

Our goal, when it's time to stretch the dough ball, is that it must have reached both the right maturation and leavening. The problem is, these two actions need different timings to occur.

How can we make sure they happen together instead?

We can control the maturation only to a certain degree, since it depends on the kind of flour we're using. So we can choose our flour and, consequently, a shorter or longer timing, that's it.

Luckily we have much more control on the leavening.

---

[10] *Unless the previous day you were ridiculously busy and you had no leftover dough balls, in that case you would use the dough you made the very same day.*

In fact, it depends on the activity of the yeast and we can actually influence it through the temperature. Yeast thrives when the temperature is between 20°C and °40C, but it slows down dramatically at around 3°C.

That's why we professionals place our dough balls in the fridge: we want to slow down, if not stop completely, the rising process.

The maturation will continue regardless of the temperature.

When we take the dough balls from the fridge they will start to rise again since the yeast slowly awakens from its nap. Managing correctly this procedure is a matter of experience and probably a little trial and error will be necessary. But that's worth the effort because the resulting pizza will taste better by all means.

Keep in mind that if you want to follow this procedure while using plain flour, most likely you will end up with a fragile dough ball. In fact, we know that plain flour matures relatively quickly.

That's not a big deal as long as you are careful and delicate enough when you stretch. Probably is not going to be easy to get a nice and round shape, but in the end your first goal should be to bake a pizza that tastes good.

You could take care of the appearance only later, when you will be a bit more experienced.

However, that's another reason why I suggest using a strong bread flour to make your dough. As you know, it will take longer for this flour to mature and this means it will take longer for it to become so fragile that it needs some special care.

Following the procedure described above and using a strong flour, you will get a very good dough ball, easy to work with and not reluctant to be stretched.

This way of preparing your dough it's an easy thing to manage for you: today you will spend around 15 minutes kneading the dough you will eat tomorrow. You can even do it while you watch an episode of your favourite show. Then, tomorrow, it will only take another 15 minutes for you to stretch and bake.

***

As you may imagine, when you are a professional who works in the pizzeria, making dough is not the only thing you do. Every menu boasts many choices, thus a whole lot of ingredients must be ready when it's time to cook for the customers.

Consequently, a significant chunk of any pizzaiolo's working shift will involve the preparation of those toppings. We should not be particularly concerned about being as quick as a professional is. I mean, in our homes we would probably have to slice, for example, only a few mushrooms rather than one whole box.

However, the way we will manage the toppings is still something we need to consider. That's because of the way we cook pizza, or to be more precise because of the temperature our oven can reach and the consequent baking time.

In fact, at the same temperature, different ingredients will have different cooking times.

For example, think about peppers: they are quite "fleshy" and are unlikely to reach the right degree of cooking by the time your pizza will be ready to eat.

The same applies to aubergines or potatoes or pumpkins.

The opposite applies to mushrooms or cherry tomatoes instead, they would most probably be overcooked, and they would shrink and shrivel.

So you definitely need to do something to avoid one of your toppings being more cooked than the other. Sure, I don't want to exclude that this could be an element you were actually looking for. But usually this is not too common and in general a uniform cooking is a more sought after feature.

The main takeaway here is that you need to know your ingredients!

You don't have to be a seasoned chef, you only need to be aware of the different cooking times and act consequently.

What to do then?

Do what a professional does, of course: cook some of the toppings beforehand. The aforementioned peppers and potatoes would be the first that pop into mind. If you roast one batch, you could use just a handful to top your pizza and use the rest as a side dish for the next day's dinner, for example, or for another recipe you are going to cook later.

A different solution would be to slice them very, very thinly, so you would be reasonably sure that they will be fully cooked when your pizza is ready.

By the way, further on you will read Chapter 5, the one about topping and cooking your pizza. You will see some more expedients there and I will consider some more ingredients.

The preparation of the toppings is for me quite a nice phase of pizza making.

When I cook at home, it's the last thing I do before I bake, and I do it in such a relaxing environment. I like to play some music and sing along with my favourite songs while I slice and chop.

The worst that has ever happened to me is that my neighbour has knocked on the door to protest about the volume being too high. Once he dared to say that I was out of tune, but that's clearly because he doesn't understand what real art is.

Working in the pizzeria, the preparation stage is a totally different league though.

A scary thing I sometimes dread, especially the day after a very busy service, when you look at your containers and you notice they are all sadly empty. In that case the prep phase becomes a race against time, while the clock that hangs on the wall is looking at you mockingly. You can almost hear the little coward laugh at you, while you run back and forth like a Tasmanian devil trying to do 725 things at once.

O, the accidents that may occur when you're trying to push too hard.

Every little distraction may be fatal. Maybe you could even grab from the lid a big jar of sundried tomatoes in oil, forgetting that you had already unscrewed the above-mentioned lid. Maybe you could spill the greasy content of that jar all over the floor, as well as over your trousers and probably your undies.

And maybe at that point the clock would be actually laughing loud at you.

If all of this would have really happened, that would have been the worst day of my life. But luckily the clock was definitely not laughing.

Come on, it was just a clock!

5

YOU'RE GETTING THERE

Life in the pizzeria can be pretty hectic and exciting.

There are those days when you finish your preparation perfectly in time, if not a little bit early, and you feel fine because everything is running smoothly. At that point you only need to wait for the first hungry person to come into the shop, or to place an order on the telephone.

Then you wait.

And you wait.

There's an unsettling silence and the atmosphere is eerie. You walk back and forth, double- and triple-check your containers, keep the oven temperature under control, so you keep yourself busy.

Oh, finally! A nice couple comes in!

They sit down and take a look at the menu and, just a few seconds later, the phone rings.

Then somebody walks in and asks for a quick takeaway pizza. Oh, the phone rings again!

Look, two more people come into the pizzeria!

This is the story of that day when you suddenly got busy, within one minute.

Orders keep flowing, both by phone and from people popping into the shop. Only five minutes ago you were chatting with your colleague about the finale of Game of Thrones, and right now the only flames you can think about don't come from a dragon, but from your oven. And possibly by yourself, because you're running faster than light to please the starved customers as soon as possible.

Situations like this are less infrequent than you think, but you need to get used to it.

There is a common saying among people who work in the kitchen, including pizza makers.

We say we are all crazy.

And I think I know where this comes from: the abrupt acceleration you are often subjected to, makes you want to shout and run away.

When I prepare pizza at home, the atmosphere is certainly different.

It's never frenetic, even if I have many guests. Family members and/or friends are here to eat, sure, but they will not complain to me if I'm running seven seconds late.

They will let me do my things and bake their dinner in peace. Actually they are always curious and they like to watch a professional at work. Sometimes they ask me if they can try themselves, so I quickly explain to them how to stretch their dough ball.

Basically, I show them the very same technique I teach people attending my pizza making classes, and they often end up signing in.

And now I'm going to describe this technique to my reader.

We will try to stretch a dough ball in order to get a round pizza, as similar as possible to the ones we usually buy from our favourite take-away restaurant.

Probably, we will not be able to get a round pizza, the first time we try.

Honestly that still happens to me, from time to time, even after years of experience and hundreds of thousands of pizzas.

But look, if the taste is good, who cares about the shape?

Don't give too much importance to the shape right now, it will come with experience.

The first step is to grab your rolling pin, take a photo of it, upload it to your local marketplace website and sell it. Exactly, you will not need this tool to stretch a pizza. Although even in Italy there are restaurants where the pizzaiolo uses a rolling pin, they offer a different product with certain features.

Certainly, using it is a hack to stretch the pizza base in a quick and easy way, but you would blow all the bubbles and totally lose all the gas produced during the rising. You would end up with a flat, tortilla-like final product...We all love tortillas, but we're discussing pizza making here!

So let's start dusting our table with a bit of flour. It could be a good idea to have some semolina at hand for this purpose.

In fact, its grains are bigger and our dough ball will "slide" on it more easily.

Now we are ready to stretch, rigorously by hand.

We start with our fingers though.

Mind you, I said "fingers", not "fingertips". If you put your fingers vertically on your dough, you only get holes and pits.

We want our base to be as even as possible, so it will cook evenly too.

Push the dough ball with your fingers using their whole length. Don't be too gentle, but don't be a wrestler either, the base must still be stretched. Try to "follow" the way it opens and try to keep the shape round.

Turn the base upside down, rotate it 90° and repeat the movements.

If the base it's a bit shy and it doesn't seem to react nicely, you don't need to try harder. Just leave it there for a while and start again. This way the gluten will relax and the dough will be less reluctant[11].

You can use this trick multiple times, if need be.

Just be careful, as your base could dry up a bit if you take too long, consider covering it with a cloth if you want to repeat this move.
The presence of the flour on your table helps you during this operation, but you don't want any of this flour to go inside the oven. Or, at least, you want as little as possible.

That's why we need to shake it away from our base.

Probably you had the chance to see some pizzaiolo, live or on video, juggling his pizza, tossing it, throwing it in the air and catching it on the fly. Pretty spectacular! That's not an end-in-itself show off, though.

Many pizza makers do their moves because they actually stretch the pizza base that way. At the same time, that's a really effective means to get rid of the excess of flour. They have the same goal as us.

---

[11] *Beware though! If this happened, I'm afraid you used too much flour and you didn't follow my instructions closely.*

Of course I'm not implying that you need to learn how to become a pizza juggler, unless you want it.

You only need to grab your pizza base by the edge with your left hand and lay it on the palm of the right hand[12].
Then pass it on the left hand again and repeat this gesture several times, at your pace. You will see that your base becomes wider and, at the same time, you are shaking away the excess of flour. Two birds with one stone, just like the professionals do. Good job, chef!

This manner of shaking flour away is the same I follow myself and I think it's pretty common in the professional world, in endless variations, since I find it pretty effective.

When my teacher showed it to me, I had to figure out by myself the exact movement that would have suited me better. You will do the same, you will find your very own movement, the one that comes more natural and feels smoother for you.

***

---

[12] *Of course you should do the opposite if you're left handed*

Speaking strictly about stretching the dough ball, the overall method I use is slightly different. It involves spinning the base on the table and letting it hang from the edge, so the gravity helps me.

However, I can't help but let some flour fall down on the floor and it would happen the same to you.

That's why I don't usually explain this method: I want your kitchen to stay as clean as possible and also I want you to spend more time having fun with pizza making, than cleaning because of it.

Leave this kind of playful exercise to restaurants' staff.

They need it to let go of the tension they accumulate during the evening. I was told that throughout the service I look like a cyborg, I'm bossy and I'm thoughtful. But when it's time to clean, even I become less serious and more cheerful and chatty.

To be honest I'm not sure if this is a good thing, because more than once somebody took advantage of my relaxed state and made me the target of their jokes.

From throwing flour on my hair (as if it's not white/grey enough already), to splashing water on my back. And I'm talking about a BUCKET of water, not just a few drops.

"Take advantage until you can, boys! Tomorrow I will be a nasty dictator again and I'll beat your back with a rod as usual, aargh!".

Only joking of course, I don't beat anybody with a rod. I use my bare knuckles.

But I am digressing here.

We have only stretched one pizza and we already want to clean? I don't think so, we still need to put the toppings and we have to bake and, most importantly, eat.
Also, let's go back into our house, where we will not proceed exactly like they do in the pizzeria. As we know, their oven is way more powerful than ours.

This is what leads us to the expedient of cooking our pizza in two rounds.

Let's turn the page and learn about this.

6

TIME TO BAKE

I'm sure you've already seen how a pizza oven is made.

Usually it is a very big piece of equipment, consisting of a large brick dome and a pavement covered with refractory stone. It must be built by skilled labour, who knows how to handle the special materials used for the design.

These ovens are able to reach and maintain correctly the high temperature needed to bake a good pizza. The average time spent in the oven is typically around three minutes if the temperature is around 320°-330°C.

However, each restaurant has its own interpretation of pizza, so the temperature and cooking times may also vary. For example, a traditional Neapolitan pizza stays in the oven for just 60-90 seconds at a temperature between 430°C and 480°C.

These temperatures are reached powering the oven with different kinds of fuels: wood, electricity, gas. As you probably know, the oldest and most traditional cooking method is wood firing. Electric ovens are also common, and gas ovens are spreading rapidly, thanks to their cleanliness and practicality.

There is an old, ongoing debate about which cooking method is best or gives the best pizza.

Since we are here, I will give you my two cents: I think that to cook a pizza it is enough to bring it to a certain temperature and we don't care which fuel has brought it. But I won't go further, I don't want to take an active part in this discussion.

At the end of the day, this does not concern us, since the oven we have at home does not offer us any choice regarding fuel.

The only thing we could actually choose would be the temperature, but to be honest we don't really have an option here. In fact, not having the opportunity to reach the performance of a professional oven, we can only try to get as close as possible to it.

Obviously the result will be different, but still satisfactory if we're using the right measures.

Let's switch on our oven then, remembering that pizza likes it hot, as we have already seen. If we want to achieve that special "crunchy-outside-soft-inside" texture we need to cook as fast as we can.

We are going to ask our oven for its best performance and we will crank it up to the highest temperature it can reach, whichever it is. At some point that little light on the front panel of the oven will turn off, meaning that the temperature we've set has been reached. Regardless, we will keep heating for an extra ten minutes.

Remember, always preheat the oven for at least half an hour.

Finally, the oven must be set to "static", not "fan", or you will get a dry pizza. Not "crispy", not "crunchy", just DRY.

While you are waiting for the oven to get super hot, you should set all the rest up, so you will be ready when the temperature is right.

Let's do a quick recap: your dough ball is by now at room temperature and your mozzarella it's already cut and has lost its excess water. Your peeled tomatoes are chopped and squashed[13].

All your toppings are ready, the tougher ones pre-cooked or sliced thinly.

We're all set. The oven is scorching. The time has come!

Let's dust our surface with some flour. We can be generous, as we now know the technique to shake away the surplus from our base. Then we stretch the dough ball using the moves we've seen in the previous chapter.

Finally we add some tomato sauce: usually five spoons are enough for a 12" base, but I leave this to your personal taste. Try not to exceed six or seven spoons though, otherwise your pizza will be too moist and it will not cook evenly.

We're now ready for the first cooking round and we will bake this "red base" we've got, no toppings but tomato sauce[14]. The more "naked" our pizza is at this point, the better and faster it will cook.

---

[13] *Its preparation is so quick you can even do it last minute, as I do.*
[14] *If your recipe doesn't call for tomato sauce, you will start baking the*

Moreover, even with the highest temperature we can afford, our pizza will stay inside the oven for a relatively long time, up to ten minutes. Many of the toppings we typically want to use would dry up if they bake for such a long time. Just think about ham or pepperoni or mushrooms...they all would shrink and lose their texture and taste.

Let's now put our red base into the oven, placing the baking tray straight at the very bottom, let's call it "the floor".

Why is that?

Because that area of the oven it's extremely hot at this point, and it will stay hot for several blessed seconds after we place the tray on it.

This means our base will start to cook pretty quickly thanks to the physical phenomenon called "conduction": the floor of our oven and the base of our pizza are in direct contact, therefore the heat will be transferred from one to the other.

The cooking time will be the tricky part here.

Every oven has its own magic and different brands' appliances could cook differently from one another, even if you set the same temperature.

"naked" base, drizzled with a bit of olive oil.

However, I will try to give you some guidelines.

The highest temperature I've seen near the knob of a household oven is 275°C (527°F). This is not bad at all, you would be able to cook your red base in around three minutes.

The opposite case is the oven whose maximum temperature is 220°C (428°F). Using this oven the first round could even last twice as long, around six minutes.
Considering these two situations as extremes, we can work out anything in between: for example, at 250°C (482°F) we would bake for around four, four and a half minutes.

Consider using this very useful tip: almost every oven comes with an included dripping pan. We can use it as we would use a baking stone[15] and leave it inside the oven while it preheats.

Again, it must be positioned as low as possible, ideally directly on the "floor" of the oven. If you use this trick, you should place your stretched base on a chopping board covered with a sheet of parchment paper, as easy to slide

---

[15] *I'm not a big fan of baking stones and, by the way, I said I don't want you to buy anything extra!*

inside the oven as it is to remove after the first cooking round.

Once the first round is up, we take the red base out from the oven and we add the rest.

"The rest" means just mozzarella if we are planning to prepare my dearest Margherita, of course! Someone likes to add a couple of basil leaves. If that sounds like you, I would recommend adding them before the mozzarella, so it will prevent them from burning and becoming sour.

You can even add them on top of the baked pizza, so they will release their flavour right there. When I bake for myself though, I never add any basil, because I really don't like it. Now I need to go, sorry, I have to give back my Italian passport...

***

Jokes apart, the way we should treat basil suggests how we could treat several other toppings. I'm referring to the more delicate ones, those that become dry and/or shrink after just a few minutes inside the oven.

First coming to mind: ham or salami/pepperoni.

When they are thinly sliced I would put them underneath the mozzarella so they would stay nice and juicy. If the slices are thicker, you can even put them on top, they should be ok. Same for the super common white/closed cup mushrooms. You would probably buy them whole and so you would be totally in control, since it's going to be you slicing them. Personally, I would not slice them too thinly because I like to see them on top.

If you are going to use pre-cooked toppings, like the aforementioned peppers, potatoes, aubergines or pumpkins, put them on top of the mozzarella. Do the same for onions, garlic, olives, capers, anchovies, sweetcorn, sausage, pancetta, cheeses in general.
I'd like to make a separate mention about spinach, because I had the chance to use them in different ways.

In a certain pizzeria I used fresh "Baby spinach" and I put them straight on the base, underneath the mozzarella. Somewhere else I cooked them super quickly beforehand and put them on top. When I use them for my home baking, very often I follow a third path and I put them on top of my pizza after I cook it.

Now that you have figured out an order to place your toppings on your pizza, it's time to finish cooking it.

Here starts the second round inside the oven, which could last anything in between two and four minutes, depending on the temperature. The rule of thumb would be to wait for the mozzarella to melt. However, if you find that the crust of your pizza looks overcooked for your taste, by the time mozzarella has melted, then next time you should consider slicing it into smaller pieces, or thinner slices.

The opposite is also true: if the crust is not well done but the mozzarella is already melted, try bigger pieces. Either way, make sure to buy the same brand, as different brands can melt differently, maybe quicker or slower.

See? Making pizza is easy, even making "good" pizza is easy.

But there are many elements, many little things you could - and should - know about. Once you are able to manage them all, you can really go to the next level and surprise your friends by giving them something that not even some "real" pizzerias would be able to offer.

It is said that the devil is in the details, and this is true for pizza making too.

The last devil's details will be the ones you're going to take care of *after* the pizza is finally baked. Again, I'm referring to toppings, the list is not finished yet.

There are a few of them you are not supposed to cook, either because they would not resist a journey into the oven, or simply because they would taste better when they are raw. I already mentioned a couple of "leafy" ingredients: basil, which should be placed under the mozzarella, but it is also great to add raw after baking, exactly like its close relative, basil pesto, which I think must be added after baking, since it's a condiment that's not supposed to be cooked; then I mentioned spinach, which I like to add raw if they are the so-called "baby" spinach.

Same goes for other leaves, the most common of them is probably rocket, but I had the chance to use lettuce, cress, microgreens and a few sprouts as well.

Some meaty stuff must be added after cooking.

The ingredient par-excellence is cured ham, the raw one many call "Parma ham". That's not wrong, but Parma ham is just one of the many known varieties[16]. No matter which kind you bought, just don't cook it, otherwise it will become so salty you will need to drink a barrel of water.

---

[16] *Some well known italian cured hams are "San Daniele", "Modena", "Bassiano" and my absolute favourite, "Norcia".*

Lately I've seen a wider diffusion of a particular kind of ham: it's called "Speck" and it's cured with salt, pepper, spices and smoke. Try it, it's pretty good, but try it raw!

Finally I want to mention "'Nduja" (pronounced "ndoo-yah" or "ndoo-ja", your choice), a kind of spreadable, spicy sausage that comes from Calabria, the region I was born in.

It's usually made with two parts of meat and one part of chilli peppers and we like to spread it on a slice of toasted bread. You can also use it to add a "special something" to many recipes, including a nice plate of pasta. Here in London it's already well known, but it's *spreading* fast and it's ready to take over the world.
Unfortunately, the most common way it's used in restaurants is the wrong one: baked in the oven. The problem is, being made with high percentages of fat, it tends to burn. If your favourite pizzeria offers a pizza with this special ingredient, ask them to put it after they bake.

In the end you won't find 'nduja at any supermarket, so the staff should be indulgent. Beware though, the pizzaiolo could swear at you for this kinky request, unless he/she is from Calabria. In that case you will probably get a free drink and a new friend.

Fishy pizzas are slightly less common than meaty ones, but still they exist. I'm really fond of salmon myself and I like to lay those slices of pink happiness on top of a freshly baked pizza.

If I plan to use prawns or shrimps, I would still add them after baking, but I would cook them briefly beforehand. That said, you can also bake them with your pizza, but they would shrink a lot, probably they would not be too appealing.

Finally, you could contemplate using some beluga caviar soaked in Dom Perignon champagne, just like some creative pizzaiolo did in Dubai. I will refrain from suggesting anything here, if you can afford it, you can do what you want!
Last but not least, cheeses.

Yes, there are cheeses that you'd better put after cooking. I'm referring to the aged ones, like Parmigiano-Reggiano[17] and its brother Grana Padano. They have harder grain and they are not creamy, so you can make some shavings using a simple grater or a potato peeler. This way, they will

---

[17] *"The name "Parmesan" is often used generically for the same cheese made outside the traditional areas of production in Italy, although this is prohibited in trading in the European Economic Area under European law."*

maintain a certain texture that will blend nicely with other ingredients'.

They also give a nice appearance...you know, you start eating with your eyes and when there's something good looking on your plate you're off to a good start.

But we are not starting at all here! Quite the contrary, we're done.

Of course I can not include here all the ingredients in this world because this would be beyond the scope of this book. But you can find me on my social networks accounts and ask me questions, I will gladly share my experience with you.

Head straight away here:
www.youtube.com/FabioulousPizza
www.facebook.com/FabioulousPizza
www.instagram.com/FabioulousPizza

Come on now, your pizza is on the plate, it's warm, fragrant and wrapped on a nice, smokey haze of loving scent.

It's time to eat, finally, buon appetito!

7

JUST DOUGH IT

We've come to the end of our journey.

We repeatedly bounced from the pizzeria to our kitchen, bringing a new detail with us every time.

We discovered that flours are not all the same and that, as a result, we have to treat them in different ways. Hence, we are now able to make a nice dough by hand, no matter the type of flour we are using.

We know which is the best tomato to use and we know the method to make the best out of mozzarella.

We manage all our favourite toppings very well and we know we need to lay them on the base in the right order, at the right time.

Oh, and that base? We are confident enough to stretch it out by hand, since we sold our rolling pin long ago.

What's missing then?

Well, just a little bit of experience and some curiosity.

Although I gave you many evergreen tips and tricks that were useful one hundred years ago and will still be useful in the future; although you are about to read my own recipe, the same I used myself to bake endless pizzas, this doesn't mean you should always stick to the same, identical routine.

I think that, if I would teach one recipe to ten people, they would end up with ten different versions.

It's ok if you shy away and find your own way and your own pizza. Feel free to "break the rules" just for the sake of seeing what happens.

Do the exact opposite of what I said or tweak my suggestions a bit, and see what happens to your final product. Use less salt and top your pizza with fruit or chocolate spread or custard or whatever you fancy, if you have a sweet tooth.

Maybe you could add a little bit of flour or reduce its amount instead, or try all the different kinds you can find on the shelves of your favourite shop and blend them with various proportions.

Then buy new ingredients, combine familiar ones with exotic stuff, play with contrasts in taste, colour, dimensions. Find your special medley and be proud of it.
In conclusion, have fun and explore all the opportunities.

If you want to discuss ideas or share opinions, please stay in touch with me through my social networks: I will be more than happy to share my knowledge and I would be even happier if you show me your masterpieces.

I'm now giving you the exact pizza-making procedure I have been following for years. We will prepare one dough-ball and we will stretch it into a pizza around 12 inch size (31/32 cm), the typical average size of your favourite pizza place.

With the doses I'm providing, the resulting dough-ball will be slightly heavier than the ones used by professional pizza makers in their restaurants. They are good at stretching pizzas, they do it countless times every day, hence they can easily reach a certain size using less dough.

As you get more experienced and comfortable in stretching the base, feel free to reduce the amounts of flour and water to get a smaller dough ball. Don't forget you can take advantage of my dough calculator here: bit.ly/doughcalculator.

Please note, I am definitely not using volume measurements here, because they are trickier to use in pizza making, and I want to explain to you why. Think about flour: one cup of all purpose weighs 128 grams and it will call for a certain amount of water, measured in cups. This same amount of water mixed with one cup of strong bread flour, would result in a very hard dough. In fact, one cup of this kind of flour weighs 135 grams. If you still want to use cups, you need to factor in this element.

The doses, now!

100 grams water, room temperature
150 grams strong bread flour (or 160 grams plain flour)
5 grams table salt
1 gram dried yeast (active or instant/quick, it doesn't matter)
OPTIONAL: 3-4 grams extra virgin olive oil (in this case it's ok to say, "one teaspoon", you got me!)

In a bowl, pour the water and dissolve the yeast in it.

Add half of the flour and mix well using a fork or a spoon, until you get a smooth, creamy consistency. Now you can add the salt and continue mixing. Add the rest of the flour in two or three rounds, but don't forget to set aside a few grams: later on they will turn out useful to "clean" your hands.

Once you have added all the flour, incorporate it nicely into the dough keeping the momentum going. I would suggest going on with your fork or spoon until the dough becomes less sticky, but feel free to use your hands. Or better, *hand*. You should always try and keep one hand as clean as possible, in case you need to grab another container, or maybe some tissue, or if the postman rings the bell.

Whatever you are using to knead, tool or hand, you must avoid squeezing, squashing, stretching, pushing and twisting.

In Chapter two, I have already described a certain movement you should get familiar with. Go underneath the dough and fold it on itself from the bottom up, maybe with a little help of your thumb. You want to push the edge you're handling into the centre of the dough ball. Then rotate your dough 90 degrees and repeat the movement with another side of the dough ball.

Then rotate your dough 90 degrees and repeat the movement.

Then rotate your dough 90 degrees and repeat the movement, over and over...

This may be easier done than said and you may definitely benefit from watching me doing it, rather than explaining it. This is why I shoot a video course, after being asked so many times. Check out a mini promo on my YouTube channel, just copy into your browser this: `bit.ly/YTfabiocourse`

If you plan to use olive oil, you should add it after all the flour is incorporated, when the dough still needs some kneading.

Remember to test it, from time to time, gently pushing your finger in it. if it springs back, then you're good to go, otherwise you will need some more elbow grease.

Once your dough is ready, let it rise in the bowl for at least eight hours at room temperature (three to four will be enough if you're using plain/all purpose flour).

The container doesn't need to be air tight, but place it where it will be safe from drafts. If you wish, spread a few drops of oil on your container before you put the dough in it, so it will come out more easily.

For the same purpose, bread bakers like to use corn flour or rice flour.

Remember, we're kneading only one dough ball. If you are making a bigger batch of dough, you need to let it rest for around one hour when you finish kneading, then divide it in as many single dough balls as you need.

Now, since the rising time could be pretty long, you could think that it's tricky to fit pizza making on your average working day.

But consider that when you knead nicely and your flour is good quality, you can increase the leavening time and expand it easily to twelve hours.
This means you can knead before you go to work, for example, and let your dough rise all day long. When you come back, it will be ready for you to stretch it and bake it.

Another solution could be to prepare the dough one day in advance. As you know, you could use the fridge, after all.

So tonight you will prepare your dough, let it rest for an hour and then stick it in the fridge. Don't forget to divide it!

Tomorrow, once you get home from work, take the dough from the fridge and let it reach room temperature. Your fridge's temperature should be something between 6° to 10°C, so a couple of hours should be enough.

8

RECIPES

While you wait for your dough to be ready, have a look at the following recipes. I have tested them repeatedly and I love them all.

I wanted to respect the menus that are not "mine" anymore, so I have decided to keep out of this list all those pizzas I have baked multiple times in the restaurants I have worked in.

You will see some of the stuff I like to cook at home for myself: some custom interpretations of classic, common recipes, as well as several creations which, to my knowledge, are absolutely personal.

Many of the toppings are quite standard and easy to find on the shelves of your favourite supermarket. A few of them are probably trickier to find and you will need to dig deeper into the marketplace, or maybe visit a local deli shop. Sometimes the smallest ones reveal pleasant surprises.

By the way, you will find that most of the ingredients I propose here are kind of poor. I have nothing against more expensive or luxury food, on the contrary. I just like something different on top of my favourite meal ever.

Come on now, let's see if I can inspire you a little bit!

I have two favourites (Margherita doesn't count) pizzas between the classics. The first one is "Ham & mushrooms". The taste of these toppings is kind of mild and they let stand out the flavour of a nice dough. However, sometimes I feel like eating something with a certain character.

That's why, to make my rendition, I have swapped the classic toppings with their "enhanced" version: smoked ham and chestnut mushrooms (they are also called "Cremini"), on a tomato and mozzarella base. That's really yummy, I promise.

You can call it "Yum" and mushrooms, if you want, as I do!

My second favourite between the classics is "Four cheese". Quite the opposite of the previous one, taste-wise! This pizza usually has a strong flavour, although this may depend on the exact blend of cheeses used by the pizzaiolo. In fact, there is not a defined mix you are supposed to use.

I'm sure that any menu that boasts a "Quattro formaggi" reveals a different combination. My menu, the one I keep in my head is no exception. My own, personal cheeses are: blue stilton, smoked scamorza and Parmigiano-Reggiano. Again, on a tomato and mozzarella base.

The acidity of the tomato is paramount to wash away a bit of the greasiness from your mouth. You should add the Parmigiano-Reggiano, in shavings, after you bake, so it preserves a bit of its consistency.

I was born in a seaside town, where you can eat fresh fish everyday, so how come fish does not take my fancy? I don't know and I don't mind. The fact is, I only like a couple of "things" that cut through water.

First, cruise ships. You can probably find a pizza on a cruise ship, but the opposite would be unlikely, so let's continue.

And then there's salmon. Even though it has actual fins and scales, I don't think about it as "fish", rather I see slices of happiness. It already tastes phenomenal on its own, but if you add it, with courgettes and pink pepper, on top of a white pizza (it means without tomato sauce), then it's total bliss.

Living in the United Kingdom, I'm lucky enough to have a Pie whenever I want. I love those pastry dough treasure chests, whether they are filled with savoury ingredients or sweet...or maybe both. In fact, I had the chance to try one with sausage and cranberry sauce and it was absolutely delicious.

Since I can't make pastry dough, I thought I could have transferred that deliciousness on top of a dough I can actually prepare, perhaps adding my personal touch. When you eat sausages, it's pretty common to use cabbage as a side dish. That's what the missing element was! My newborn pizza had crumbled sausage, purple cabbage and cranberries. The latter give the necessary acidic touch, so you wouldn't need any tomato sauce here. Hence, the base has to be white.

As you have seen, I sometimes get inspiration from the food I eat. I basically try to "pizza-fy" something I enjoy.

Being a massive fan of Mexican cuisine, whenever I can I head to my favourite place to savour certain flavours and see certain colours. Trying to bring them in my field came quite naturally at some point. So one day I woke up and decided to put red onions, red kidney beans, crumbled tortilla chips and guacamole on a tomato and mozzarella base.

The result is nice and flavourful and the different textures blend together amazingly. Some heat would be a nice optional. Chipotle flakes work quite well, but being a chilli head, I'd rather use some Habanero, way hotter.

I like contrasts, not just when it comes to food, actually I'm full of contrasts myself. I think that, having in your mouth opposite flavours and consistencies, really enhances your eating experience. I don't usually enjoy any sweetness when I eat my pizza, but if I add a contrasting element the perspective changes.

To make this recipe a little bit of extra preparation is needed, but it's worth it. You will sauté some butternut, diced in cubes, with salt, black pepper and a pinch of nutmeg. Then you will sauté a mix of mushrooms of your choice with garlic and rosemary. Finally you will put them on a tomato and mozzarella base, and add some crushed hazelnuts. There's sweetness, heartiness, freshness and crunchiness. That's Fabio-ulous.

One more thing I like about living in the UK, is the astonishing number and variety of local cheeses available on the marketplace. Cheddar is only the most famous, probably. My first choice will always be the mighty Blue Stilton, which I have already mentioned. However, a recent discovery made it to my podium and it's the Cornish Brie, which I like better than the original from France (it's just a matter of personal taste...*excusez-moi, mes amis*).

I looked for a good match for a while and I think I've found it in another unquestionably local foodstuff: bacon. I cook it beforehand and then I put it on a tomato and mozzarella base. The last bit of its fatty part will melt and stay there, blending nicely with that lovely cheese and producing a remarkably "Brie-tish" kick.

If you want to try this one, then it's time to head to a Deli Shop and see if they sell 'nduja. Since it's a hot thing, it's nice to pair it with cheese, whose fatty part will soften the heat a bit.

A combination I've seen on several menus is the one with "Burrata", a particular mozzarella stuffed with heavy cream and mozzarella shreds. It's not too common to find Burrata at the supermarket, but you're already going to the Deli Shop, so see if they have it there.

By the way, I'm here to cover the worst case scenario, that's usually my case. I can't find Burrata anywhere around me, so I came up with a substitute: my pizza is made with 'Nduja and cottage cheese, on a base of tomato and mozzarella, and it's delicious.

Our round up finishes with a pizza that is not a pizza. Calzone is well known right now, but let me give you a few details.

It's a speciality food prepared with the same dough ball you would use to make a regular pizza. You need to stretch it as usual, but actually that's the one and only circumstance where I would allow the use of a rolling pin, at least until you're not experienced enough to get your base nice and even.

There are both the baked version and the deep fried one, usually smaller in size. In this case it's very common as a street food.

The filling may vary from region to region and from city to city.

However, the creativity of the pizzaiolo will be absolutely relevant, hence if you want to try yourself, feel free to use whichever ingredient you want.

Ultimately, I want to pay tribute to the Neapolitan tradition and mention their version: ricotta, salami and mozzarella. Many times there's also cracked black pepper and almost always you will find a layer of tomato sauce on top of the calzone itself. That helps to prevent the surface from burning.

The calzone I'm suggesting you here is stuffed with ham, ricotta, spinach, mozzarella and a few pieces of peeled tomatoes. I like to brush the top with a little bit of extra virgin olive oil and finally I bake at 250°C for 9/10 minutes.

Frequently Asked Questions

Please note, the following it's NOT meant to be a complete, final list.

This is only a round up of several questions I often had to reply to. You can use it like a quick and easy reference guide. If you have a question that's not included here or on my YouTube channel, don't hesitate to keep in touch and ask me, via my Facebook or Instagram accounts.

Q: *Why is my dough hard?*
A: Because you used too much flour, try to reduce the amount next time. If you are using my recipes, chances are you tried to knead on a floured surface, next time resist the temptation.

Q: *Why is my dough spread flat?*
A: Because your gluten is not strong enough, next time try kneading longer.

Q: *How do I know my dough is kneaded enough?*
A: Gently push your finger on the surface, if it springs back, then it's ready. Otherwise you will need some more elbow grease!

Q: *Why does my dough smell like alcohol?*

A: Because you have used too much yeast and you're now smelling some over-fermentation. Some of it will disappear with baking, but some will stay. Next time reduce the amount of yeast.

Q: *Why is my dough not rising?*

A: There are many possible causes:

1) you killed the yeast using hot water, next time use room temperature water;

2) you mixed yeast and salt together, next time keep them separate;

3) your yeast is expired, next time check it beforehand, see next question;

4) You used too much flour and now the yeast is struggling to "pump" the dough;

5) The temperature of the room is very low, the ideal one is above 20°C. Try putting your dough inside the oven with the light on, or inside the microwave after you heat a glass of water for one minute.

Q: *How can I check if my yeast is still ok?*

A: Put a teaspoon into a glass of lukewarm water, ideally around 30°C, add a teaspoon of sugar and wait around 10 minutes. A nice froth should now cover the surface. If it doesn't, then your yeast is not active anymore.

Q: *I'm sure I used the right amount of flour, why is my dough so sticky?*

A: I'm afraid you forgot the salt. You're still in time to add it, but you will need to be patient because, at this point, it will take time for the dough to absorb it. It would be easier to add more water too, and then more flour accordingly, to re-establish the balance in your dough.

Q: *How do I know my dough is ready/has risen enough?*

A: Quick & easy test to check: once again, gently push your finger in it, if it springs back, then it's not ready yet. Let it rise longer. When a trace remains, then you can stretch it.

Q: *Can I freeze my dough?*

A: Yes, you can. Remember: move it from the freezer into the fridge the previous day, so its temperature rises slowly. Then take it from the fridge at least a couple of hours before you use it, it must reach room temperature.

Q: *Why does my dough shrink back when I try to stretch it?*

A: There are a couple of causes:

1) You have used too much flour, next time try to reduce the amount or just follow my recipe;

2) You didn't let it rise enough, the gluten needs time to decay, please refer to the maturation times I explained in Chapter 1.

Q: *Ok, but at this point I need to stretch it, what should I do?*
A: Let it rest for one minute and try again. It will relax and it will be less reluctant. You can repeat if needed.

Q: *Why is my pizza soggy?*
A: If the top looks ok, nice colour and melted mozzarella, then you probably put all the toppings on your base at once, preventing it from cooking evenly. Please refer to Chapter 5, when I explained about the "red base". Also, remember you always need to preheat the oven.

Q: *Why is my pizza watery?*
A: Chances are you have used some fresh mozzarella straight from its bag. Next time remember to dry it, as explained in Chapter 1. Also, ingredients like mushrooms may release some water when you cook them, next time try to reduce their amount.

Q: *Why is mozzarella burnt and toppings have shrunk?*
A: Again, you put all the toppings on your base from the start. Next time start with the "red base".

Q: *Why do I drink a lot after I eat my homemade pizza?*
A: There are several possible reasons:
   1) You're pizza is undercooked, the obvious fix is to leave it in the oven longer, next time;

2) Too many toppings, ingredients, condiments. If you stuff your pizza with three kinds of cheese, pepperoni, onions, chicken, ham, pineapple and your pizza weighs one kilo, then you will overload your stomach and the poor thing will struggle to do its job;

3) You were too generous with the yeast. The highest allowed amount is 5% of flour's weight. Use it sparingly next time, and follow my suggestions.

Q: *Is there any way you can teach me more?*
A: Sure! I already mentioned I shot a video course where I dig deeper in some topics and you get to see me in action. Just type into your browser this: `bit.ly/YTfabiocourse`

Q: *Why is my pizza so bloody good?*
A: Because you have read this book and followed my teachings to the letter!

References

How to fold calzone

bit.ly/howtofoldcalzone

Why I don't mix salt & yeast in my pizza dough!

bit.ly/yeastexperiment

How to choose the right yeast?

bit.ly/chooseyeast

Why is my dough not rising?

bit.ly/doughnotrising

The Bread and Flour Regulations 1998, United Kingdom

http://www.legislation.gov.uk/uksi/1998/141/contents/made

Canning Tomatoes and Tomato Products

https://nchfp.uga.edu/how/can3_tomato.html

The official DOP Consortium site

https://www.mozzarelladop.it/en/

What's in your water?

https://www.thameswater.co.uk/help-and-advice/water-quality/whats-in-your-water

Influence of commercial baker's yeasts on bread aroma profiles

https://www.sciencedirect.com/science/article/abs/pii/S0963996913001749

How to impact gluten protein network formation during wheat flour dough making

https://www.sciencedirect.com/science/article/abs/pii/S2214799318301966

Yeast is Fussy About Temperature

https://www.exploratorium.edu/cooking/bread/yeast_temp.html

World's Most Expensive Pizza

https://www.langlaisservices.com/worlds-most-expensive-pizza/

The Consortium of Parmigiano-Reggiano

https://www.parmigianoreggiano.com

The Disciplinare of Verace Pizza Napoletana

https://www.pizzanapoletana.org/images/file/disciplinare%202008%20UK.pdf

Made in United States
North Haven, CT
07 August 2023

40041920R00071